I hear its whirring engine
Glimpse its dipping wing
Against the sun-filled cloudless sky
Of early evening

A little flying poem
That circles down to land
On the runway in my head
And the page beneath my hand.

Every
was
once

Allan Ahlberg

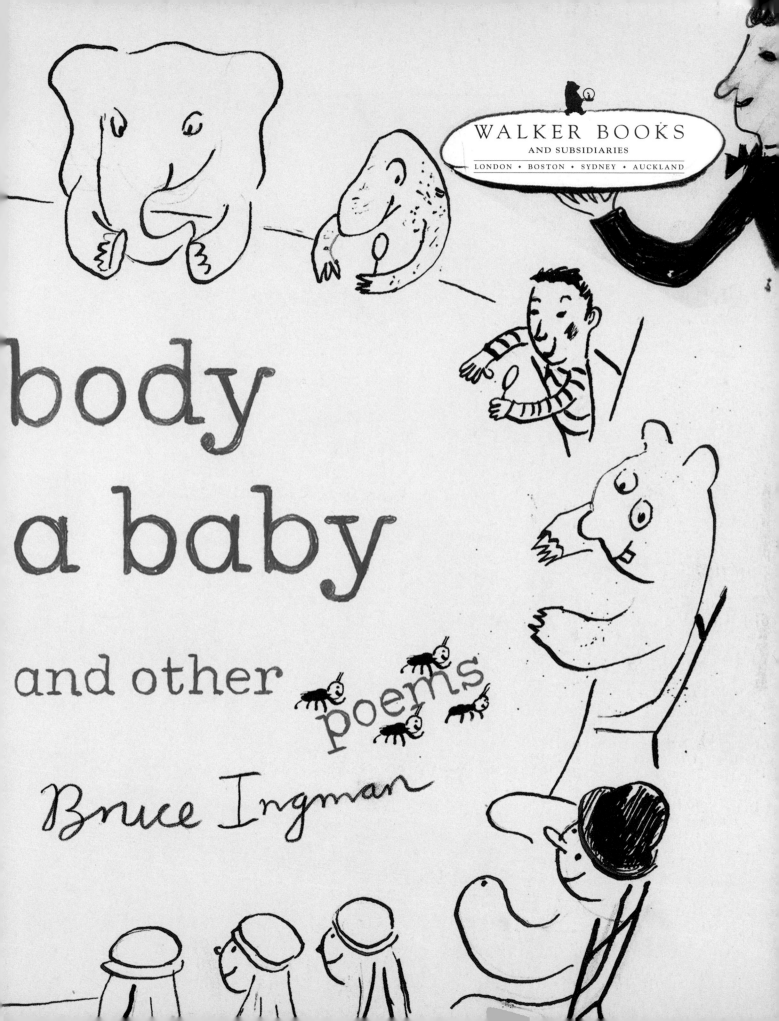

body
a baby
and other poems

Bruce Ingman

WALKER BOOKS
AND SUBSIDIARIES
LONDON • BOSTON • SYDNEY • AUCKLAND

For Alvie, Ted and Ramona
MANY THANKS TO EMILY, DAVID AND DANIEL

First published 2010 by Walker Books Ltd
87 Vauxhall Walk, London SE11 5HJ

This edition published 2011

10 9 8 7 6 5 4 3 2 1

Text © 2010 Allan Ahlberg
Illustrations © 2010 Bruce Ingman

The right of Allan Ahlberg and Bruce Ingman
to be identified as author and illustrator
respectively of this work has been asserted
by them in accordance with the Copyright,
Designs and Patents Act 1988

This book has been typeset in ITC Slimbach
Cover title from a typeface by A2/SW/HK

Printed in China

British Library Cataloguing in Publication Data:
a catalogue record for this book is available
from the British Library

ISBN 978-1-4063-3000-7

www.walker.co.uk

The following poems are reproduced by kind
permission of Puffin Books Ltd, London:
"Elephants v. Insects", first published in
Friendly Matches, Viking, 2001; "A Happy
School" and "Everybody Was a Baby Once",
first published in *The Mrs Butler Songbook*,
Viking, 1992.

Contents

Monday Is Washday 6

(∗) Dirty Bill 10

When I Was Just a Little Child 12

If You Meet a Witch 16

Summer Snowmen 18

Nativity 24

Dinah Price 26

(∗) The Sausage Whistler 30

(∗) Small Hairy Mouse 32

Dangerous to Know 34

The Good Old Dolls 36

A Happy School 38

Monster Munch 40

Little League 46

Cinderella 47

Elephants v. Insects 48

The Lizard Man 52

Everybody Was a Baby Once 54

The Ping-Pong Song 58

Friday Is Fishday 60

(∗) Shut the Shutter 64

Monday Is Washday

Monday is washday in our town
Washday, sloshday
Squeeze-and-squash day
Rubday, scrubday
Put-in-the-tub day
Hang-on-the-line-and-let-it-dry day
Mother-the-soap's-gone-in-my-eye day!
From morning till the sun goes down …

Monday is washday

in our town!

Dirty Bill

I'm Dirty Bill from Vinegar Hill,
Never had a bath and never will.

When I Was Just a Little Child

When I was just a little child
The world seemed wide to me.
My Mum was like a feather bed
My bath was like the sea.

My highchair was a mighty tower
The view I had was grand
With cups and plates stretched out for miles
Across the tableland.

When I was just a little child
The world looked tall to me.
The stairs rose to the mountain tops
My Dad was like a tree.

My Dog was like a big brown horse
With bits of white and grey
And sometimes with a little help
He'd gallop me away.

If You Meet a Witch

If you meet a witch
Don't scream and run
Whatever she does
It's only in fun.

If she turns you
Into a frog – don't croak!
She's only teasing
It's only a joke.

If she sends you to sleep
For a year or more
Don't bat an eyelid
Just smile – and snore!

If she pops you
Into a pot – keep calm
Don't get in a stew
She means no harm.

But – if she pulls out a bib
And cries, "Yum, yum!"
Then scream the place down
And run home to Mum.

Summer Snowmen

In the good old days
When snow was snow
Snowmen lasted years, you know.

They kept cool heads
When the sun came out.
They didn't melt, they ran about.

They took their holidays
By the sea
And paddled, just like you and me.

When wintertime
Came round again
They piled the snow
and made more men.

Still, that of course
Was years ago
In the good old days when snow was …

snow.

Nativity

Keith's forgot his royal crown
Kevin's late (again)

Jason's lost his frankincense:
The Unwise Men.

Dinah Price

I see Dinah Price
Climbing up a tree.
"Climbing's fun," Dinah says.
And I agree.

I see Dinah Price
Swinging on a gate.
She says, "Come and try it –
Swinging's great!"

I see Dinah Price
Sliding on the ice.
I think slides are magic …

So does Dinah

Price!

The Sausage Whistler

One day a boy went walking
And walked into a store
He bought a pound of sausages
And put them on the floor.

The boy began to whistle
He whistled up a tune
And all the little sausages
Danced around the room.

Small Hairy Mouse

A man having dinner at Crewe
Found a small hairy mouse
in his stew.

Said the waiter,
"Don't shout
And wave it about
Or the others'll want one too."

Dangerous to Know

Don't wind him up
He'll do you harm
The Man with the Keyhole
Under his arm.

The Rubber Girl
Without a doubt
When rubbed up wrongly
Will rub you out.

Plughole Person
For just a frown
Will spin you around
And suck you down.

Don't cut up rough
When they are near
Or the Scissors Ladies
Will clip your ear.

If you mean to live
As long as you can
Don't get on the wick
Of Candle Man.

The Good Old Dolls

We are the old dolls
Losing our hair
Hats and dresses
The worse for wear.

We are the old dolls
Noses worn
By little girls' kisses
Before you were born.

We are the old dolls
We sit or flop
In the Old Dolls' Home
Or the Oxfam shop.

We are the old dolls
Fingers broken
Old food still in our mouths
Last words spoken.

We are the old dolls
Worse for wear
The little girls who loved us
No longer there.

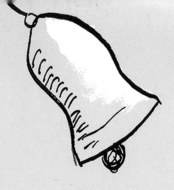

A Happy School

There was a happy school
Long, long ago
High on a mountain top
Lost in the snow.
Oh, how the children ran
When they saw the chestnut man
Hot chestnuts in his pan
Long, long ago.

There is a happy school
Far, far away
Where they have strawberry pie
Three times a day.
Oh, how the children shout
When the teachers serve it out
There'll be seconds, have no doubt
Far, far away.

There is a happy school
Up in the sky
Waiting for all of us
To come by and by.
Oh, how the angels yell
When they hear the dinner bell
Something's cooking they can tell
Up in the sky.

Monster Munch

Monster breakfast
What's to eat?
Tadpole toasties
Dreaded wheat.

Monster dinner
Mouldy greens
Graveyard gravy
Human beans.

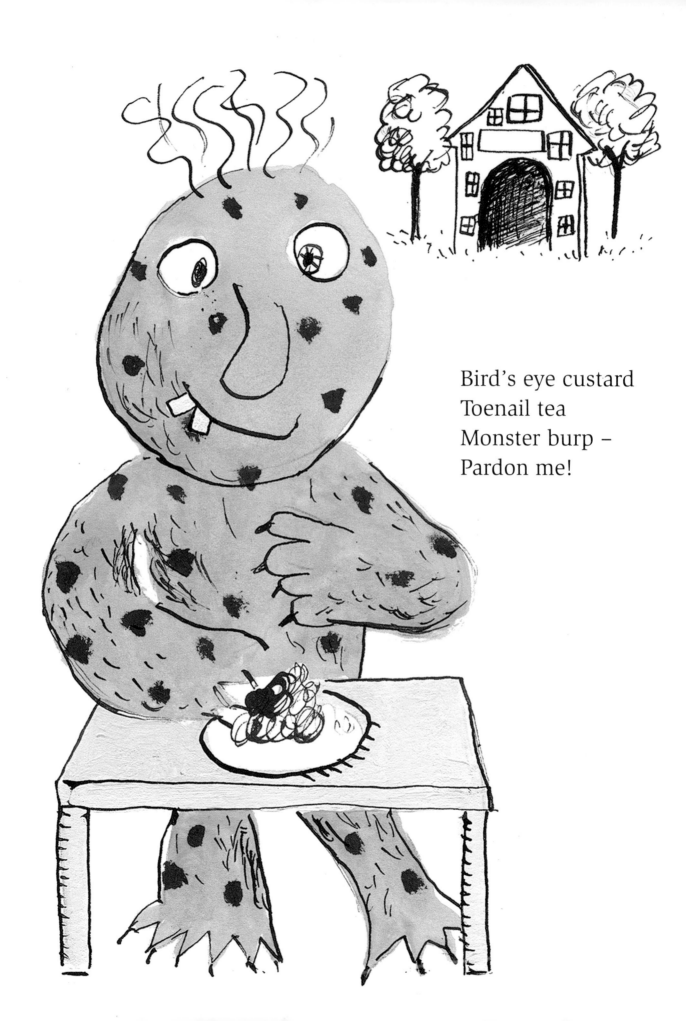

Bird's eye custard
Toenail tea
Monster burp –
Pardon me!

42

Monster party
Monster cake
Eat the candles
Tummy ache!

Monster medicine
Monster spoon
Three times daily
Get well soon.

Little League

Little Tommy Stout
Put himself about.

Little Bo Peep
Collapsed in a heap.

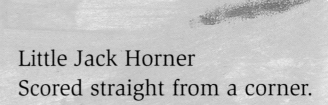

Little Polly F.
Complained to the ref.

Little Jack Horner
Scored straight from a corner.

Cinderella

Poor Cinders never makes the team
Got no idea at all
She wears glass trainers half the time
And runs away from the ball!

48 Elephants

The Elephants and the Insects
Came out to play a match
They trampled in the jungle
Till they'd cleared a little patch.
They scuttled round and trumpeted
Just glad to be alive
Until the half-time whistle
When the score was 15–5.

v. Insects

The Insects in the second half
Brought on a substitute
A modest little centipede
But, brother, could he shoot.
He ran around on all his legs
Beneath the tropic sun
And by the time he'd finished
Well, the Insects, they had won.

"Oh, tell us," said the Elephants
"We're mystified indeed
Why wait until the second half
To play the centipede?"
"That's easy," cried the Insects
As they carried off the cup.
"He needs an hour
to sort his boots …

The Lizard Man

With scaly skin and curly comb
The Lizard Man is coming home.
His wife and lizard children wait
To meet him at the garden gate.

They take his briefcase, grasp his claw
And lead him through the open door.
There's worms and curried frog for tea
And *Super Lizards* on TV.

The Lizard Man removes his shoes
He reads the *Lizard Daily News*
Sips a glass of Old Swamp Whisky
And pets the cat, who's acting frisky.

His little daughter wanders by
She flicks her tongue to catch a fly.
His baby son begins to wail
The dog has trodden on *his* tail.

The Lizard Man takes off his tie
He's happy but he can't tell why.
Come rain or sunshine, hail or blizzard
It just feels … fine, to be a lizard.

Everybody Was

Everybody was a baby once
Everybody was a baby once
Everybody went to beddy
With a little furry teddy
Everybody was a baby once.

a Baby Once

The baby comes first in life's great plan
Everyone started out small
The child is father to the man
The race begins at a crawl.

Oh, your daddy was a baby once
And your mummy was a baby once
Yes, your daddy and your mummy
Used to sit and suck a dummy
Everybody was a baby once.

Friday Is Fishday

Friday is fishday in our town
Fat-fish, flat-fish
Cod- and cat-fish.
Catch 'em, dry 'em
Batter-and-fry 'em.

Serve-on-a-plate-with-a-pile-of-chips day
Pass-the-salt-and-smack-your-lips day
Thank-you-please-and-have-some-more day
Ma-my-bread's-gone-on-the-floor day!
From morning till the sun goes down …

in our town!

A woman to her son did utter
"Go, my son, and shut the shutter."
"The shutter's shut," the son did utter
"I cannot shut it any shutter."

The End